Level Up!

How to excel at every level of the engineering
career ladder while staying true to yourself

By Rebecca Leung Comsa

For my son, Rafael.

Contents

Introduction

Every career is made up of different stories.
Do these stories sound familiar?

Joe is a star engineer at his company and spearheaded leading-edge designs for a world-famous product that millions of people use every day. After a decade of feeling great about his contributions to his field, financial success and being seen as an industry leader, he has not been promoted at all and is getting bored at his job. He longs for a change but every internal lateral application he makes is denied without a satisfactory reason. Why does no other department want him? Joe longs for the novelty of the early successes he had when he was a lead programmer but is reticent to give up his benefits, stock options, not to mention his friends and reputation that he grew over his tenure. He wonders what he can do to move forward. Should he change companies?

What about this?

Sarah thought she was doing everything right. Her boss loves her and, after finding success as a junior engineer, and in project and product management, she was given an engineering team to manage. From day one, she set strong standards on how the work should be done based on management techniques that were effective in her previous roles, but she is struggling with her new position. Each engineer needs so much of her time to train to her high standards and there are times when she just wants to stop explaining and finish the work herself. She can envision the solution so easily; why can't her employees? She cannot seem to get a good understanding of why her employees do not seem to have the same spark as she does for the work.

Her first project was a success, meeting all milestones and KPIs with gusto, but she can sense something was wrong with the team by the second and third major projects. Somehow, morale is not where it should be, and people are lackluster at team-building events. She gets her first 360-degree performance review from her team and the anonymous feedback was atrocious - not one person said anything positive about her as their manager. Worst yet, she is sure that she knows who wrote each comment. She does not know if she can treat her employees the same after what they wrote about her. Over the course of six months, she loses several star employees and she is unable to fill the role internally. She needs to turn this team around and fast.

And what about this last story:

Chris has had a great 10 year run as an engineering executive. He has now been promoted to the Head of Operations and the transition has hit him hard. Whereas his engineering and quality teams were a natural fit for him, his new operations teams seem to never click. Every attempt Chris makes to engage with the team just results in stilted answers and eye rolls. Chris needs to succeed in this role for him to reach his ambitious goal of being the Chief Operations Officer of a Fortune 500 company. With all the issues he has been having, his attention is no longer on his lofty goal, but on whether he will be able to keep his current job! What can he do to improve this situation?

Like Joe, Sarah, and Chris, thousands of people with engineering backgrounds struggle every day to get noticed by their superiors and be promoted into mid-level or senior management. A good portion of those people never make the vertical move; and a good percentage of engineers who get promoted into management actually fail, wallowing in poor performance and anxiety for years until they are restructured or terminated.

Whether Joe, Sarah or Chris' stories resonated with your personal experience or you have heard similar stories from your network, I hope you are picking up this book because you are vowing to not let your current role be the end point of your career.

This book is not about rehashing how talented engineers struggled to become and then failed as people managers. This book aims to move you past the old stereotypes about the poor people management skills of engineers and give you the real-world skills that you need to get you to the next step of your engineering career. This will equally help junior engineers in their first internships and mid-career engineers to navigate the workplace to achieve the career you desire.

Who is this book for?

You are picking up this book because you have experienced the above situations yourself. Or you have the foresight to want to ensure that you do not fall into a career-limiting trap. It is not uncommon for engineers to want a new challenge after a prolonged tenure at a company and wish to pivot into a new role. Unfortunately, it is not always clear what skills you need to move to the next phase.

As I was writing this book, I heard from countless people - friends, family, neighbors - who confided to me about having trouble achieving their career goals. They report getting pigeonholed in a technical field, unable to move forward in their profession, all the while watching others move ahead.

The truth is what got you to your current role will not get you to your next dream position. Here is a tough lesson at this point in your career: the skills that got you to the current stage of your career might not get you to the next step on the ladder.

This is not a personal failure on your part. This is the first time you've ever prepared for the following act. This book will help you develop the new skills you need to succeed.

This book is not for someone happy in their role. If you are content with your current career progression and wish to go no further, then you may give this book to someone else in need. There is a lot to be said for engineers and programmers who are honestly content in their current roles and wish to go no further.

Why I can help

I am a professional engineer with nearly two decades of managerial experience. I became an engineering manager within eighteen months of starting my career, and one of my greatest joys is to coach my teams to achieve their career goals. I have coached dozens of mentees and employees into supervisory roles and watched with absolute pleasure as they succeeded. It should be noted that fast-tracking into engineering management is not common within a traditional engineering career stream and I had leapfrogged many intermediate roles.

To this day, many of my friends who wish to become managers in their field are still struggling to do so even after more than a decade into their professions. The reason why I was able to move forward in my career in a traditional engineering field so quickly was that, in addition to observing my friends, I came from a family full of engineers. This allowed me to spend my life observing the ups and downs of their careers. As a result, I was able to note career-limiting traps that they or their colleagues have made prior to embarking on my own journey.

As such, I have spent my entire life watching engineers develop, problem solve, and create. But I have also watched these same engineers create design flaws, spend a lot of resources solving problems that do not move the needle, or create unsupportable solutions. And I have certainly watched generations of engineers make poor management decisions and not take care of their teams or corporate expectations. Engineers are talented, but their base skills are not immediately conducive to people management. Engineers need to be managed in an environment that can direct their ability to problem solve constructively.

As I became an engineer and later an engineering manager, I struggled with these issues myself. I completed my MBA after my undergraduate degree and then, after graduation, researched and practiced management techniques. I have struggled with the classic engineering personality, resulting in the blunt method of communication, the endless need to sweat the small stuff, and the ego that comes up if there is even a small framework built into their day. I have had tough performance reviews where my engineering team loved me, but the internal stakeholders did not and vice versa. My teams have also had these issues that I learned to - and sometimes failed to - manage where I couldn't reach the humanity inside my employees to motivate them.

After a lot of soul searching, I had to check my ego and get an executive coach. This coach taught me how to interact with my team members, set better boundaries and expectations, and strengthen my communication skills. She taught me how to motivate my team, work with multiple types of personalities, and essentially how to be a leader that my employees would love while helping them reliably produce the work that my own managers are expecting. With her help, I have gotten promoted faster than before and achieved a milestone that I had desired for a decade. More importantly, I have set more realistic expectations for my at-work relationships.

I was so inspired by my experience with the executive coach that I wanted to give my employees the same level of mentorship. I started making a point of watching for and researching examples of strong managing and coaching styles. I am convinced that there are special skills needed to manage engineers effectively and this differs from managing other professions. On the flip side, I am equally convinced that engineers becoming managers need specific coaching to be effective motivators of people. By overcoming these issues, I was able to get closer to becoming the engineering manager I want to be, and I want to share this knowledge with you.

What you are going to learn?

This book will help engineers who just got promoted to people management or want to get promoted but cannot figure out how. This book will provide a science and data-driven roadmap for STEM-based professions to easily move into a managerial role. After reviewing managerial and research-driven literature, each section of this book will review the latest organizational and managerial theories applicable to managing as an engineer and then take you through self-reflection exercises to move your thinking forward.

To get you to the next steps in your career, in chapter 1, we will first walk through what are the differences between a single contributor and a manager. We will also discuss why you may want to become a manager, versus staying in the single contributor role and what are the benefits of each. Next, we will discuss the roadblocks that are stopping an engineer from being promoted and what this means in your career.

In chapter 2, we look at the environment in which engineers typically work. We will look at how engineers are placed in a company, their department's goals, their typical career path, their typical psychosocial profile, and the role they play in their organization.

This is then contrasted with the roles and responsibilities of other departments in chapter 3. This chapter goes into the organizational structure of how other departments are organized, as well as how their department's goals and incentives compare with that of the engineering department.

In chapter 4, we look at the typical engineering personality. This will help us understand and name specific characteristics of the engineering mindset and helps us set the stage to understand the similarities between the engineering department and the other departments in a company.

We then get into the mindset of each of the departments. Chapter 5 discusses the typical career paths and organization motivation of the other departments.

While the organizational structure may inform how each department works, in chapter 6, we are going to look at how each department *thinks.* To do this, we are going to look at a concept called the Big Five Personality traits and compare these traits between a typical engineer and the people he or she will work with.

Now that we have looked at the environmental factors affecting an engineer at work and the mindsets of the surrounding people, we are going to look at developing new communication and working styles to help you be successful in each of the departments. Chapter 7 will review verbal cues in the workplace, while chapter 8 will follow up with non-verbal communication methodologies. We are going to review examples of communication at each level and the expectations of the audience.

Now that we have reviewed the working environment and the communication requirements to be successful in a workplace, we are going to apply this and start improving your day-to-day performance at work. Chapter 9 will start this process by showing you how to be a successful single contributor as an engineer in a way that puts you closer to a promotion and continue forward. All the tools essential to making the move to management will be given.

Now that you know what you are in for, let us get down to business!

CHAPTER 1

Understanding the Challenge

I want to start this book by complimenting you on acknowledging that you have goals greater than your current role and performance. This means you have both the ambition and the humility to recognize that you need to level up to the next step of your career. I know that this is difficult to do. It takes a lot of bravery and self-reflection to admit that you *currently* do not have the skills to move forward the way you envision for your life. I sincerely believe that this book can help you achieve your dreams!

The second thing I want to say to you is that *you are not alone.* Thousands of engineers out there have had a hard time transitioning from a single contributor to a people manager or the head of a department. Many fail to even be given the chance, and while others fail after being given the opportunity.

This is important because, in a lot of cases, if you are interested in staying with the company, you will need to meet the challenge quickly after a promotion by improving your management skills. Some companies do provide a way out by giving you the option to get demoted back into a single contributor role. However, this is not guaranteed.

Before we get started, I want to point out that there is no shame in admitting that perhaps you do not want to be a manager of any kind. There are a lot of talented engineers out there that become subject matter experts in a niche area, are lauded as the best of their industry, and never send a day of managing people in their careers. A single contributor career path can be extremely rewarding. Being a people manager can also be frustrating when embarked upon with the wrong expectations. But if you feel like there is something inside of you that is pushing you towards management, this book aims to help those who wish to take the incredibly rewarding managerial path.

What is a single contributor?

Let's start with some definitions.

When you start your career, you rarely start as a manager. Instead, you start as what is called *a single contributor.*

This term means you are responsible for your work only. You are responsible for finishing the product, the workmanship of your deliverables, and completing it all within the approved deadline. This deadline is typically tied to a budget your manager must follow. Depending on your work situation, you may have to ask for the appropriate levels of help and training. You may be given projects increasing in technical complexity, but do not give you additional personnel or financial responsibility. Progression is usually indicated by numbers (Business Analyst I, Business Analyst II, Engineer I, Engineer II, and so forth) or by prefixes (Junior Engineer, Engineer, Senior Engineer). What is similar in all these roles is that you are not responsible for managing other people.

There is some confusion about the project manager title and whether they are managers due to their job title. Indeed, if they do not manage a team of other project managers, then they are not true personnel managers.

Now, even though you are a single contributor, you are still responsible for many things.

Single Contributors are responsible for technical work

First, you are responsible for your work. You are responsible for producing good work that is appropriate for your skill level, your tenure, and pay. Your work will be benchmarked against that of other employees and within the industry. This workmanship requirement extends to administrative work that may be outside of your discipline, such as reporting, providing updates, and clerical work. These tasks are just as important to complete as your core work, as these tasks help your team organize itself, communicate its efforts to executive management and contribute to marketing your team's finished product to other parts of the organization.

Single Contributors are responsible for being pleasant employees

Second, you are responsible for your attitude. Emotional intelligence is important in any role. While it is important to produce good work, you must present it in a way that makes both your manager and your peers happy. Despite many television shows like *Big Bang Theory* or *House* that showcase STEM professionals being so good at their technical expertise that they are allowed to be rude to their colleagues and clients, the reality is that this behaviour is not allowed. If people do not enjoy working with you, this will ultimately limit your career.

Single contributors are responsible for maintaining a network

You are responsible for your relationships with other employees. As an employee, you will work in a team of people in an organization and you are responsible for the upkeep of a professional relationship with other employees, whether they are below you, your peer, or above you in rank. It is important to note that there are limits to your relationship with your co-workers that are different than that with your friends.

Single Contributors are responsible for their knowledge

You are also responsible for keeping on top of your industry. Many people believe that once you leave formal education, you do not need to refresh your skills. Most if not all jobs require you to continue your technical education and improve your soft skills.

It is also important for you to continue to learn about your industry, on top of learning about your discipline. This means that if you are an analyst working in manufacturing, it is important to grow your understanding of both engineering and the manufacturing world. This makes you more effective in your decision-making and makes you easier to promote.

Now that we know what a single contributor is, let's look at the role a manager typically plays.

What is a manager?

Studies show that one of the biggest determinations of whether you will become a manager is if one of your parents was a manager. This passes a gut check. After all, you get to see and hear about more of your parent's day than any potential mentor. The way they handle people, projects and issues at home is probably carried over from the skills they have at work. You will naturally pick up on their capabilities and mannerisms.

In my discussions with people who ask for my advice on becoming a manager, one of the first things I like to ask them is what they think a manager does. Ultimately, most people lack an understanding of executive roles and discuss only a small percentage of managerial responsibilities.

I realized that most people who don't already have mentors to help them on their career journey – whether it be family, friends or colleagues – and find it hard to know the full scope of what managers do. To make it more difficult, not all managers have the same responsibilities and you don't get to see 100% of your manager's day beyond your limited daily interaction with them. Very few people have a role where they shadow their managers for an entire year so that you can observe their full job description for a performance cycle. And even if do get to be a fly on the wall for a manager's full responsibilities, only a small percentage of engineering managers excel at their duties enough to be a worthy teacher.

But what if your parents or close network have never taken on such a role and you have no avenues to observe a manager fully at work? How would you know what managers are supposed to do? This next section will be your mentor and review the roles and responsibilities of a manager.

Managers maintains a budget for their team

This is the item that a lot of STEM professionals forget — your manager is responsible for justifying the cost of your salary and benefits. There is a huge amount of administrative work related to this–from framing out your job description to convincing the executive team that your job description is necessary for the organization. To get this approved, they must provide significant market research for the labour market and the price of such skills. After hiring, the manager is responsible on a yearly basis to ensure that they have the salary, training and accessorial budgets to meet their organization's goals.

Managers distribute work

Managers plan, organize, direct, and control resources to achieve company goals. They also must decide if they have enough manpower to get the work done. Managers at lower levels get work streams from their superiors and they break it down to deliverables that the teams can complete. Managers remove resourcing, technological, and political obstacles from completing your work.

Managers are responsible for the work output of their teams

Managers are responsible for your output. They check your work and review it for quality before submitting it to the client or upper management. When you make a mistake, it is ultimately your manager's responsibility in the eyes of the executive team.

Managers develop the team culture

A great manager sets the tone for his or her team. One of the most important things a manager must do is manage the team's energy. This starts from hiring for the right people, encouraging and coaching staff to be their best and supplying all resources for your employment. They are also responsible for communicating internal and external changes to their employees and ensuring that the changes are implemented.

Managers facilitate interpersonal relationships

Separate from the above, managers also resolve interpersonal conflicts and handles escalations. Should an employee be unable to move forward in a conversation or meet their goals due to communication opportunities with internal or external stakeholders, a manager will be responsible for facilitating and workshopping the discussions until the employee is back on track.

Managers evaluate their teams

Managers must evaluate their talent. Do they have the right person for the role? Have any roles changed and do the employees affected need training? Are employees performing according to expectations? Who deserves a merit increase? Who needs an improvement plan? Managers are continuously monitoring the above to ensure they can meet the company's goals.

Why would an engineer want to become a manager?

Now that you have a better idea of what a manager does and how it is different from a single contributor role, let's look at why you may want to level up to managerial role.

While the technical aspects of engineering are very rewarding and typically well-paying, there are a lot of reasons an engineer may want to move out of a single contributor role and into a management role.

Financial Reward

The foremost reason why engineers would like to become a manager is that, generally speaking, engineering managers have higher salaries and a stronger benefits package than a single contributor. Only a highly specialized industry leader single contributor will have a wage higher than the management team.

Contribution

Many engineers wish to reach the managerial ranks because they truly believe that they can make a difference. They believe that they can improve performance and provide a positive contribution to the organization.

Career Support

In a lot of companies you work for, particularly in the more traditional sectors, promotion into management is the method that companies prefer to award high-achieving employees. In many organizations, a manager or manager-in-training is provided with greater personal development resources and more mentorship and training. They are also likely to be given more bonuses, shares, and options as well.

Influence

Suppose you are a subject matter expert in your field. Your company needs to scale a software enhancement that impacts millions of users. How do you convince others that your solution is the best fit? How would you convince others that your project, out of the thousands of other designs other single contributors are producing in your firm, is the one to get funding? How will you convince others to work on this? Being a manager provides the influence in order to get things done.

Personal Learning Opportunities

After being a subject matter expert in your own field, perhaps you may be hungry for additional challenges. Being a manager opens you up for more opportunities to grow your soft skills like sales and negotiations and teaches you more about the other departments in your company, such as finance, legal, and compliance. You also get to stretch your skills into the strategic side of engineering at your company and get the opportunity to see the big picture.

Putting it Together

In this chapter, we reviewed what is a single contributor versus what is a manager and their roles and responsibilities. We then looked at what is needed to be successful in each role. We discussed at why an engineer may want to join the managerial ranks and the advantages and disadvantages of the role. Understanding this will help us look at the common reasons an engineer may not get the opportunity in the next chapter.

Story Time

Let's revisit our heroes from the beginning of our journey, with a focus on Joe.

Joe is a star engineer at his company and spearheaded leading-edge designs for a world-famous product that millions of people use every day. After a decade of feeling great about his contributions to his field, financial success and being seen as an industry leader, he has not been promoted at all and is getting bored at his job. He longs for a change but every internal lateral application he makes is denied without a satisfactory reason. Why does no other department want him? Joe longs for the novelty of the early successes he had when he was a lead programmer but is reticent to give up his benefits, stock options, not to mention his friends and reputation that he grew over his tenure. He wonders what he can do to move forward. Should he change companies?

Based on the story above, would you say Joe's role is a single contributor or a manager?

What is his goal?

How is his current role aligned with his goal?

Next, what do we know about how Joe has been performing to these requirements?

Single Contributors' responsibilities

Responsibilities	Rating out of 5
Completing assigned tasks to industry and company standards	
Having a good attitude	
Having positive relationships with their colleagues	
Knowing their industries	

Manager's responsibilities

Responsibilities	Rating out of 5
Ensuring their teams have everything need to complete assigned tasks	
Evaluating their teams	
Distributing tasks	
Managing payroll	
Ensuring their team stays on budget	
The energy of the team	
Having positive relationships with their colleagues	
Representing their companies in their industries	
Representing their industries	

What should Joe's next steps be? _____

Reflection Time

For this chapter's exercise, let's start off by thinking about your career so far. Identify whether you have been a single contributor or a manager. Then, for each role, rate your ability to perform the expected responsibilities out of 5 where 1 is not meeting and 5 is excelling.

Single Contributors' responsibilities

Responsibilities	Rating out of 5
Completing assigned tasks to industry and company standards	
Having a good attitude	
Having positive relationships with their colleagues	
Knowing their industries	

Manager's responsibilities

Responsibilities	Rating out of 5
Ensuring their teams have everything need to complete assigned tasks	
Evaluating their teams	
Distributing tasks	
Managing payroll	
Ensuring their team stays on budget	

The energy of the team	
Having positive relationships with their colleagues	
Representing their companies in their industries	
Representing their industries	

Next, let's look at whether you can get a managerial mentor.

Name three people whose managerial styles you admire. What do you like about their managerial style?

1. _____

2. _____

3. _____

Based on the insights in this chapter, what can you improve on in the next 30, 60 and 90 days?

Chapter Topic	30 Days Due Date:	60 Days Due Date:	90 Days Due Date:
Chapter 1: Understanding the Challenge *Prompt: What can you do to improve as a single contributor? What skills can you improve as a manager?*			

CHAPTER 2

The Roadblocks Engineers Face as Managers

In the first chapter, we have looked at what are the two major categories of employees within an organization - single contributor and manager - and how they support a company's goals. We have also discussed why an engineer may find it advantageous to move from a single contributor role to a managerial role if there is a personality and career goal fit. Let us keep it moving and start looking at the expectations that managers must fulfill and how engineers have typically failed to be considered good managers.

What makes a good manager?

Now that you have decided to become a manager, what do you need to do if you want to succeed?

If you recall from chapter 1, we discussed the main responsibilities of a manager below:

Managers are responsible for ...

- Ensuring their teams have everything needed to complete assigned tasks
- Evaluating their teams
- Distributing tasks
- Managing payroll
- Ensuring their team stays on budget

- The energy of the team
- Having positive relationships with their colleagues
- Representing their companies in their industries
- Representing their industries

Note that everything we have talked about so far is the manager's responsibilities from an organization's point of view. And yet, being a successful manager requires not only meeting the base, day-to-day expectations of the job description - there are a lot of unspoken expectations from the stakeholders as well.

So, who are the stakeholders in a manager's career? And what are they expecting from a manager? This next chapter looks at what employees and the executive team expects from a new manager.

What do engineers expect from their managers?

The first set of stakeholders for an engineering manager is the people they manage. For most engineers, the first step in the managerial ladder is to manage other technical team members, so it is helpful to have this as the first stop in our exploration.

Engineers, whether they are students, single contributors, or managers, are predominantly "convergers" in terms of how they process information. This means they like to learn all the components of a system or process first, consolidate that information into a design, and then, lastly, build once all the possibilities and risks are understood. This is a unique learning profile – other personalities like to learn by trial and error via building or skip the designing process altogether. Since this learning style differs from the way many other groups of people learn, managing engineers requires a specific managerial style to minimize miscommunication and frustration.

Let us start by looking at what all employees, in general, expect from their managers first. According to a survey of 500 U.S. employees in the book "What People Want" by Terry Bacon, employees want the following:

- Honesty
- Fairness
- Trust
- Respect

This is nothing ground-breaking. In general, employees of all types wish to be well-treated and have clear sense of where the company is headed and how they contribute to that journey. This forms the basis for any employment relationship.

But are those qualities all that is needed to effectively manage engineers?

In 2009, Google Inc. decided that they wanted to understand what would make a better engineering manager. They started a study called Project Oxygen where they data-mined performance reviews, feedback surveys, nominations for top-manager awards, and compliments and complaints. This produced a profile of the ideal manager at Google. What were the findings?

The most interesting finding is that technical expertise in a manager is not important in a people manager in even at Google, one of the most technological advanced companies in the world. Engineering employees, like their non-engineering peers, valued even-keeled bosses who made time for 1:1 meetings, were helpful, and took an interest in employees' lives and careers. They also found that managers had a much greater impact on employees' performance and how they felt about their job than seemingly larger variables, such as the mission of their company and the meaningfulness of their work.

Google incorporated these findings into their managerial training and gained statistically significant improvements in 75% of their worst-performing managers. Most interestingly, this contradicted the long-held belief at Google that managers need to have deeper technical knowledge than those they are managing.

Difficulties Managing as an Engineer

In the earlier section, we've discussed one common misconception that engineering managers must be technically stronger than their employees. Let us look at other reasons why engineers may have a hard time managing employees.

As discussed in chapter 1, managers oversee communicating and implementing changes internal and external to their departments. Unfortunately, multiple studies have found that communication is not a strength amongst engineers. As well, most engineers are only trained in technical communication in university which is not optimal for all learning needs.

Any engineering change management can be optimized through delivery in multiple communication styles. Communication patterns, timing, and perceived need for change alter the level of participative decision-making required for employee acceptance. This is especially important if the engineer is managing teams with employees with non-technical backgrounds.

If a manager has the mastery of excellent leadership styles that communicates in a way that improves employee motivation and morale, despite facing significant organizational changes, the organizational change would be met with higher levels of employee satisfaction and acceptance.

What does an employer expect from an engineering manager?

The previous section covers what your *employees* expect from you as their manager. This section will review what another set of stakeholders, your *employers,* will be expecting from you as the head of their engineering teams.

Surveys conducted with CEOs of engineering companies found that executive management are looking for engineering managers who are skilled in two different areas. On the managerial side, they expect their engineering managers to be flexible to changes in operating environments. Another expectation is to be able to navigate increasingly globalized projects and lead multidisciplinary and multicultural teams. As well, managers are expected to have the ability to personalize corporate goals for their engineering teams. On the engineering side, the executive team are looking for managers who possess deep technical knowledge despite the Google findings mentioned above.

Let's sum it up. What are all the expectations for a manager from all their stakeholders?

Managers are responsible for ...	Engineering Employees Expect	Employers Expect
Ensuring their teams have everything they need to complete assigned tasks Evaluating their teams Distributing tasks Managing payroll Ensuring their team stays on budget The energy of the team Having positive relationships with their colleagues Representing their companies in their industries	Honesty Fairness Trust Respect Even Keeled Boss Available for 1:1s Helpful Interested in their personal lives	Adaptable to operation needs Can manage large global projects Able to lead diverse teams Deep technical knowledge Ability to convert corporate goals into personal actions

If, as you are reading this, you are thinking that this is a lot to take in, truly; you are not alone. Now that we have acknowledged the challenge that engineers face in their quests to move into management, we can start digging into the solution.

This is where it gets exciting!

Putting it Together

In this chapter we reviewed the expectations that engineering managers face from above and below them in the organization. We reviewed how many of these expectations are often not well understood when engineers move from single contributor to management and how some of the expectations from the team the engineer is managing may not align with that of senior leadership. Often, a new manager may start off succeeding with only one group, but to be successful, they must master the art of pleasing both.

Story Time

Let's revisit our heroes from the beginning of our journey, with a focus on Sarah.

Sarah thought she was doing everything right. Her boss loves her and, after finding success as a junior engineer, and in project and product management, she was given an engineering team to manage. From day one, she set strong standards on how the work should be done based on management techniques that were effective in her previous roles, but she is struggling with her new position. Each engineer needs so much of her time to train to her high standards and there are times when she just wants to stop explaining and finish the work herself. She can envision the solution so easily; why can't her employees? She cannot seem to get a good understanding of why her employees do not seem to have the same spark as she does for the work.

Her first project was a success, meeting all milestones and KPIs with gusto, but she can sense something was wrong with the team by the second and third major projects. Somehow, morale is not where it should be, and people are lackluster at team-building events. She gets her first 360-degree performance review from her team and the anonymous feedback was atrocious - not one person said anything positive about her as their manager. Worst yet, she is sure that she knows who wrote each comment. She does not know if she can treat her employees the same after what they wrote about her. Over the course of six months, she loses several star employees and she is unable to fill the role internally. She needs to turn this team around and fast.

Based on the story above, what is Sarah's goal?

How has Sarah performed against her team's and her manager's expectations?

Engineering Employees Expect	Is Sarah meeting this expectation?
Even Keeled Boss	
Available for 1:1s	
Helpful	
Interested in their personal lives	

Employers Expect	Is Sarah meeting this expectation?
Adaptable to operation needs	
Can manage large global projects	
Able to lead diverse teams	
Deep technical knowledge	
Ability to convert corporate goals into personal actions	

What should Sarah's next steps be?

Reflection Time

For this chapter's first exercise, let's look at your expectations of your manager.

Write in the space below what your top 5 expectations for a manager would be.

1. _____

2. _____

3. _____

4. _____

5. _____

Now let's look at your experience. How have your managers met or missed your expectations? How have you met your own expectations?

Expectations	Has your manager met your expectations?	Have you met your expectations?

For this chapter's second exercise, let's look at how you are meeting engineering employee's or your employer's expectations.

Engineering Employees Expect	Is your manager meeting this expectation?	Are you meeting this expectation?

Even Keeled Boss		
Available for 1:1s		
Helpful		
Interested in their personal lives		

Employers Expect	Is your manager meeting this expectation?	Are you meeting this expectation?
Adaptable to operation needs		
Can manage large global projects		
Able to lead diverse teams		
Deep technical knowledge		
Ability to convert corporate goals into personal actions		

Based on the insights in this chapter, what can you improve on in the next 30, 60 and 90 days?

Chapter Topic	30 Days Due Date:	60 Days Due Date:	90 Days Due Date:

Chapter 2: The roadblocks facing engineers Prompt: What can you do to engage more stakeholders in your career? What skills can you learn to improve your competency in managerial tasks?			

CHAPTER 3

The Engineering Organizational Structure

Now that we have discussed the difference between single contributor and managerial roles in chapter 1 and the roadblocks engineers typically face as managers in chapter 2, let's look at the environment in which engineers typically work. Understanding the lay of the land is very important. It helps you unlock how the executives within your company see your department and how you \ support organizational goals. This section first looks at the organizational motivation of the engineering department and then digs into the typical career paths that engineers take within it.

One quick note before we get started: while everything we discuss below is relevant for most companies, the titles or reporting structures may be a little different. Each company has a slightly different way of organizing itself, but the general paths and job expectations should stand.

Organizational Motivation of the Engineering Department

Typical Career Path of an Engineer

Let's start with understanding the typical engineering department. One of the most interesting things about the engineering curriculum is that no part of your education tells you what your career path will be. Most graduates tend to accept a junior role within an organization as your first job in the engineering field. From there, they tend to focus on self-improvement on the technical side, but not on the managerial side. Learning about how jobs and responsibilities change with each role will help you anticipate your next step.

Let's start from the beginning of an engineering career.

Engineer in Training

If you start in a traditional engineering field in a large engineering firm or related field, you typically start with a junior engineer or Engineer in Training title. If your company is in parts of the world that have an engineering chartering system, before getting your license or charter, you cannot legally use the engineer title. At this point in your career, you are likely just performing engineering-related administrative tasks, such as note keeping, project coordinating, basic drafting, and basic projects core to your education. It would be unlikely for you to get larger, high-risk, or highly visible projects.

Engineer I - III

After you achieve your charter or license, your company can refer to you as an engineer in your title. Your skill level and tenure are demarked by suffixes such as I, II, or III. You will be responsible for minor tasks within a project. In some other cases, you may oversee a larger project where you are highly supervised. Your title may change, and the projects get more visible, but the increase in responsibility is technical only. You are not considered a subject matter expert and are unlikely to represent your company to the public.

Head Engineer / Chief Engineer

This is the last stop for a lot of engineers should they remain single contributors. This role means you have achieved technical excellence and are likely a subject matter expert in your company and within the public discourse. If you aim to be at the peak of your technical field, being a Chief Engineer is your goal. You would rarely oversee deploying financial or human resources, but, rather, your expert opinion on the technical feasibility of a situation or design would likely be the ultimate go-ahead in your company. You may also represent your company at conferences or offer your technical opinion in documents available to the public, such as press releases, public policy or in judicial matters.

Engineering Manager

This is where things diverge from single contributorship. As the engineering manager, you are now responsible for a team of engineers or related STEM professionals. You will be responsible for the performance of the team as described in chapter 1, including work distribution, team culture, budgets, discipline, and hiring and firing. You will be responsible for managing personality types and knowing how to motivate different people on an assortment of different occasions. Your manager may start you off with a smaller team and, if you are successful, you will move up to managing larger teams with greater responsibilities. Your superiors may also move you laterally around the organization by managing similar-sized teams to give you a broader understanding of the business.

Engineering Director

After several years of working as an engineering manager, you may be promoted to the director level. This promotion is typically contingent on a strong level of understanding of the technical side of several areas within the company and a strong history of success managing different-sized teams. In this role, you are now responsible for a group of managers and their reports. Your deliverables are more visible to executive management and the outside world. You now evaluate your managers on their ability to get the best out of their teams and the strengths of their deliverables.

VP of Engineering

While the director level is focused on tactics, the VP is focused on strategy. It is less about execution, but rather applying their thinking to the business and addressing the problems of the business with several frameworks. In terms of experience, a VP of engineering is usually thought of as an expert and a trusted source in their area of expertise, as they typically have had ample managerial and director-level experience in the company's major corner-stone projects. At the senior level, they contribute by working across strategic and business units. They are institutionally versatile; they have had multiple internal roles as leading managers and directors and have a firm grasp of the entire business. They can critically evaluate areas outside of their own area of expertise. They also understand externalities such as competition, the global market and can use their impact to ensure that the organization can compete in any market.

Chief Technical / Information Officer

This is the ultimate step for most technical managers. The CTO is responsible for setting the technical and engineering culture and vision of the entire company. He or she oversees all technology within the company and is responsible for ensuring the competitive advantage of the company through the lens of its technology. The CTO and the Chief Engineer are the most senior technical roles in the company.

Other Career Paths

Engineers may also jump in and out of other departments throughout their career. Typical moves out of the engineering department includes switching to operations, IT, or marketing. This can provide engineers a greater insight in the to the rest of the business world and should be considered.

Putting it Together

In this chapter, we reviewed the typical path that engineers take up the career ladder. This provides a good perspective on what to expect in your own career and allows you to contemplate which path you would like to take and the responsibilities at each step. This section also provides an understanding on the motivations of your peers and your managers.

Story Time

Let's revisit our heroes from the beginning of our journey, this time with a focus again on Joe.

Joe is a star engineer at his company and spearheaded leading-edge designs for a world-famous product that millions of people use every day. After a decade of feeling great about his contributions to his field, financial success and being seen as an industry leader, he has not been promoted at all and is getting bored at his job. He longs for a change but every internal lateral application he makes is denied without a satisfactory reason. Why does no other department want him? Joe longs for the novelty of the early successes he had when he was a lead programmer but is reticent to give up his benefits, stock options, not to mention his friends and reputation that he grew over his tenure. He wonders what he can do to move forward. Should he change companies?

Based on what we learned about the engineering career path, where would you say is Joe's current position?

_____

Given his discontent, what role do you think he is interested in?

_____

Reflection Time

Now that you know the typical career path for an engineer, for the first exercise in this chapter, write what your ultimate goals are in your career.

Now, let us break it down.

Where would you like to be in 5 years or 10 years? What title would you like to have?

	5 Years	10 Years	Ultimate Goal
Goal			

Now, using the descriptions of that role, what skills do you have? What skills do you need to work on?

	5 Years		10 Years		Ultimate Goal	
Goal						
	Skill Required	Achieved?	Skill Required	Achieved?	Skill Required	Achieved?
1						
2						
3						
4						
5						

Based on the insights in this chapter, what can you improve on in the next 30, 60 and 90 days?

Chapter Topic	30 Days Due Date:	60 Days Due Date:	90 Days Due Date:
Chapter 3: The Engineering Organization *Prompt: What can you do to improve your understanding of the engineering organization?*			

CHAPTER 4

The Engineering Personality

W e have now talked about the typical engineering career road map and the organizational motivation of the engineering department. Let's now take some time to review the typical mindset and personality of an average engineer. This chapter dives into the heart of the typical engineering professional, looking inside their brains using a framework called the Big Five Personality Traits.

We will go into an explanation of the Big Five Personality Traits, and how the average engineer ranks in each of these traits. We will also look at the average personality profile of a manager. We will then use this information later to compare the average personality traits of an engineer against the average personality profiles of other departments in chapter 5.

It should be noted that these are the *average* traits of a group and that there is a lot of variability within any major group. It would be rare for you to meet an engineer with a personality that matches the exact average. Specific individuals have unique backgrounds, experiences, and circumstances that may make them veer from the average.

Despite all this, the Big Five Personality traits are still helpful as it allows us to set the stage to compare the common differences and similarities in mindsets between the engineering departments and the other departments within the company. This will help us, in turn, improve communication within and outside of the engineering department.

Big 5 Personality Traits

Let's begin with looking at what is the Big 5 Personality Traits and why it is useful.

The Big 5 Personality Traits is the best model we must frame the different aspects that describe a personality. Personality traits are bucketed up the five basic dimensions, each being evaluated on a spectrum. The five traits are agreeableness, openness, conscientiousness, and neuroticism. These serve as the building blocks of personality. The skeptic in you may think that there are more traits to describe one's personality - and you would be right. There are other models, however, evidence largely show the Big 5 Model is the most capable of describing a personality.

Let's start reviewing the different personality traits!

Conscientiousness

People with high conscientiousness have high levels of good impulse control and goal-directed behaviors. They are considerate, organized, and good with details. They like to spend time planning and preparing. They are task-oriented and enjoy having a schedule.

People with low conscientiousness dislike structure and are more likely to be disorganized. They procrastinate and often cannot meet deadlines.

Agreeableness

Agreeableness describes the level in which a person has high trust in others, altruism, kindness, affection, and other pro-social behaviors. An agreeable person shows a great deal of care for other people and feel strong empathy. They get a lot of joy from helping others and making people around them happy.

Someone with low agreeableness doesn't seem to care about others and doesn't seem interested in other people's problems. They insult and discount others' feelings and opinions and are not afraid of manipulating others to get what they want.

Neuroticism

A person who is highly neurotic is characterized by emotional instability. This person feels a lot of stress, and worries about many things, leading to anxiousness. He or she experiences larger shifts in moods and struggles to bounce back after setbacks.

A person who is low on neuroticism deals well with stress, rarely feels sad or depressed and is more relaxed. This person is usually emotionally resilient and can handle setbacks with ease.

Openness

A person who is high on openness rates high on characteristics like being imaginative and insightful. People who rate highly on openness have a broad range of interests and are curious about the world. They are eager to learn new things and enjoy new experiences. They also are more adventurous and creative. New challenges are exciting to them, and they love tackling abstract concepts.

Individuals who are low on openness dislike change, resist new ideas or the ideas of others, and dislike abstract or theoretical concepts.

Extraversion

A person high on extraversion is excitable, sociable, talkative, assertive, and has high amounts of emotional expressiveness. They are outgoing and gain energy in social situations. Being around other people helps them feel energized. They enjoy being in the center of attention, like starting conversations, and enjoy meeting new people. They have a wide social circle of friends and acquaintances and find it easy to make new friends.

A person low on extraversion prefers solitude and feels exhausted after socializing. He finds it difficult to start conversations and dislikes making small talk. He or she dislikes being the center of attention.

How do Engineers fall into this?

Research has shown that engineers score lower on agreeableness and neuroticism and higher on extraversion, conscientiousness. The older the engineers, the more conscientious and autonomous they are. In addition, engineers who stopped their education at their undergraduate degrees are more conscientious than engineers with advanced degrees. All studies suggest that more attention should be paid to the development of interpersonal skills.

What are the Big 5 Personality Traits of Managers?

We have reviewed the definition of the Big 5 Personality Traits and how engineers stack up. Let's compare this to the average personality of a manager.

When empirical studies were completed comparing managers against single contributors in a wide range of industries, it was found that managers score higher than non-managerial staff on extraversion, agreeableness, openness and conscientiousness and were, on average, less neurotic. They also scored higher on narrow traits, including assertiveness, optimism, work drive, and customer service orientation.

So why is this important?

It has been found that three factors, extraversion, low neuroticism, and conscientiousness of the Big 5 Personality Traits have a significant effect on a manager's decision-making and management styles. These results carry practical implications for managerial staff selection, training, and career planning for engineers. If managers have a distinct personality type, then it is likely that the executive team will be looking for similar personalities when it comes to promotions.

Conversely, as a manager-to-be, you can see these as areas of improvement to get further in your career and help you find better matches for your skills based on your personality. You can work on fine-tuning one area at a time, perhaps with the help of a mentor or an executive coach. It can also help you understand why you have stayed in a specific role.

A Final Note about the Big 5 Personality Traits

While we have discussed average personalities in this chapter, it is important to note that every person is different. While engineers may have a set of average personality traits in aggregate, individual people have individual backgrounds, upbringings and interests, and motivations that would affect their ratings on the Big 5. Some engineers may be higher on the Agreeableness scale, while others may be higher on the neuroticism scale. It is important to ensure that you respect your and others' individualism to ensure a successful professional relationship.

Putting it Together

This section provided an overview for the Big 5 Personality Traits. We then reviewed the Big 5 Personality Traits for the average engineer and how their personality compares to that of a typical manager. This provides insight on how a typical engineer may differ in personality than a typical manager and its impact on an engineer's ability to meet the expectations of an executive management team.

Reflection Time

We are skipping Story Time for this chapter to focus on your Big 5 Personality Traits.

Exercise: Using the Big 5 test, find out where you fit within each of the buckets. What was your score?

Personality Characteristic	Your Score
Conscientiousness	
Agreeableness	
Neuroticism	
Openness	
Extraversion	

Are there any insights that surprise you?

Now pick your manager and think of what their answer would be.

Personality Characteristic	Your Manager's Score
Conscientiousness	
Agreeableness	
Neuroticism	
Openness	
Extraversion	

How are they different? How are they the same?

Now pick one of your peers or employees. How would they fill this in?

Personality Characteristic	Their Score
Conscientiousness	
Agreeableness	
Neuroticism	
Openness	

Extraversion	

Based on the insights in this chapter, what can you improve on in the next 30, 60 and 90 days?

Chapter Topic	30 Days Due Date:	60 Days Due Date:	90 Days Due Date:
Chapter 4: The Engineering Personality *Prompt: What can you do to align your Big 5 Personality characteristics to better align with your career goals?*			

CHAPTER 5

How the other Departments Work

N ow that we have discussed the core engineering career path and the typical engineering personality, let us spend some time discussing the people engineers will interact with outside of the engineering department.

Maintaining healthy relationships with other employees outside of your own department is very important. As a single contributor, you may be called on as a Subject Matter Expert and as you progress through your career, as a manager, your role within the organization is much bigger and you integrate into other departments' worlds. You may even become a director or vice president of several departments. As a result, learning how to work with different departments, different organizational motivations, and different personality needs will prepare for your next steps in your calling.

In this chapter, we are going to look at other major departments in an organization, including:

1. Operations
2. Quality
3. Legal
4. Sales
5. Marketing
6. Finance

7. HR

8. IT

9. Leadership

In each departmental section, we will go into the:

- Typical Career Path - the typical career path for that department

- Organizational Motivation - what is the main goal for this department? What are their deliverables and interests?

- Where your Organizational Motivation Overlap -Where their interests overlap with the engineering department

Note that there may be some departments that are not mentioned here. Depending on the nature of the industry your business is in, there may be other departments, such as customer service, logistics, or research, that support your core business. As well, this is a general overview of what each department does. There are companies where specific departments have responsibilities that deviate greatly from the rest of the industry.

Operations

Starting with the inner workings of your business, operations is how your company produce the goods or services with which it earns its principal income. It is how your company creates the bulk of its value to its external customers. For example, if your company was in food services, the operations team would oversee the production of the food.

In some cases, the engineering department may fall in the operations department. If your company is in engineering services providing designs for bridges, then the engineering team is a part of operations. In other situations, the engineering department is a support function rather than in operations. In this case, your designs may aid in the effective and efficient execution of core operations rather than be the product itself.

Typical Career Path

Operational team members typically start as agents, clerks, or line persons in a group of other individuals with similar backgrounds. The entry-level work is repetitive and repeatable. Like STEM professionals, their two main skills needed to move up the career ladder are through industry knowledge and company experience. However, they have another opportunity to move up via technical knowledge. They can also gain managerial skills over time and become people managers through internal training. Operation managers may or may not have a post-secondary education, depending on the industry, however, some companies, particularly those in specialized industries such as technology, now look for individuals with degrees and MBAs to manage their operations.

Organizational Motivation

There is a large variety of people who go through operations. Most of their day is spent delivering results in a transactional manner and firefighting at the supervisory levels. They are typically assessed and awarded by their throughput or their team's throughput, and quality.

They are likely to be on a shift-based schedule, improving with seniority. They may go through a large part of their careers without taking Christmas or special holidays off, so if they get the chance, they guard their earned privileges carefully.

Operations also have more issues related to volume-related failures. Whereas you may have periodic computer crashes that may slow you down on your design or project deliverables, system failures mean they cannot meet quotas, resulting in financial penalties.

Where your Organizational Motivation Overlaps

Engineering and operations have overlapping motivation in areas of strategy and execution. If you are in a field that generates the operational ideas for execution, operations may depend on your team for new products, new methods for assembly, manufacturing, delivery, or new organizational ideas. In other situations, engineering may be a support service where you provide input for specific projects. In both situations, you need to have the whole of operations on your side.

Time is always a big factor. Unless they were specifically scheduled, operations do not have time to look at the big picture through projects and strategic exercises. Where engineering professionals and executive level employees have time to trial and error to perfect their designs, operations do not have this luxury, as they are incentivized by time and unit related KPIs. An initiative that does not have a quick and visible benefit may be coldly met by operations.

Quality

The quality department oversees ensuring that the products and services your company produces meet internal and external quality standards. They ensure the company's management system and processes can enable the organization to deliver products and services that meet defined quality criteria.

Typical Career Path

The quality department has a similar career path as the engineering department. New hires start as quality analysts and move up to lead and managerial roles. Post-secondary education is not necessary, however, there are several quality certifications that a professional can achieve.

Organizational Motivation

The quality department's main motivations are to meet quality key performance indicators and satisfy internal and external auditors.

Where your Organization Motivation overlap

A lot of industries and organizations are required to or choose to be compliant to quality management system standards such as ISO 9001. A part of these standards contains requirements that are specific to an engineering or design department. Typical parts of the design process that are required in the QMS standard are controlling design input, configuration verification, and documentation.

Sales

The sales (or the business development) department oversees all the activities that lead to your company's goods and services being sold. These activities include sourcing prospects, improving industry reputation, becoming trusted advisors, and providing customers with solutions. Within an organization, the sales teams may be divided by products, lines of business, customer profile or geography.

Typical Career Path

Sales typically have a more diverse background than engineering. One does not need any specific educational background to join sales, although many who specialize in technical sales may have a degree in that area. Sales skills are typically learned on the job, however, there are courses available to sharpen your talent.

Sales professionals may start their career in an entry-level junior sales or sales administration role, then move into a Sales Executive position in a couple of years. They can be in either internal sales, meaning working to increase sales with existing customers, or external sales, working with companies that are not current customers.

Organizational Motivation

Sales employees ultimately are trying to increase or support the sale of the organization's goods or services. The team is partially or entirely paid in commission, and may be subjected to sales quotas, depending on the company structure. The team is ultimately motivated by pushing forward and closing sales and ensuring that their customers are happy so that they return. They will do what it takes to get customers through the door and will try to push operations to meet their customers' requirements.

Where your Organizational Motivation Overlap

Sales typically want to deliver what they promised to the client, however, they may not get into the details of the execution by operations. If you are in engineering, you will often have to design or provide an ad hoc solution to something that would help the salesperson close a deal while still adhering to the company's design and quality standards. You may also support the vendor intake or service delivery processes and the sales team will push you to commit to specific delivery times.

It is very much worth your time to get to know your company's sales department as they hold valuable insight on the problems customers are facing and what parts of your designs they value. Depending on the organization, sales may be very far removed from the operational and engineering staff. There are a few engineers I know who have never met their sales talent. Getting to know them at company events may push your ideas and career forward.

Marketing

The marketing department is responsible for creating campaigns for the organization to generate leads and prospects for the sales department. The department researches customer insights and profiles, then builds a strategy to best reach, educate and persuade that prospect that your company is the best answer to their opportunities.

Typical Career Path

A conventional career path for a marketing employee is to start as a marketing coordinator. Other titles for this role would be market specialist or account coordinator. These employees assist with research, customer service, administrative tasks, and reporting to account executives. Once this is mastered, the next step is typically a marketing manager. This role requires additional leadership to execute a marketing strategy and establish processes while mentoring entry-level employees.

Using market research and reports from managers on market conditions, marketing directors adjust the overall strategy to increase purchase intention and brand equity. Past this point are the VPs of marketing or the CMO (Chief Marketing Officer). These roles are often the spokespeople for the company and are required to work across departments to strengthen the companies' products and services. They are responsible for heading all areas of marketing, and ultimately responsible for the ROI of marketing initiatives in the company.

Organizational Motivation

Marketing is a product-driven department that tries to understand what the customer needs. These people do the work of trying to find new products to create, understand the demand and business case of the product.

Where your Organizational Motivation Overlap

There is a considerable amount of area where marketing and engineering overlap. Both departments have product-driven mindsets. Marketing will be looking for support by engineering in the product's creation, manufacturing, and execution by operations.

Areas where engineering and marketing may have tension, would be the market feasibility of the product. Many engineers love to build interesting and technically challenging products, but marketing may reveal that there is no market for the goods or services.

Finance

Finance is a broad term that involves institutional financial, corporate finance, public accounting, and banking. Each of these has its own subcategories, including private equity, portfolio management, research, treasury, business intelligence, and valuation. Not all of these functions are within a company. The finance department in a typical company is in charge of raising funds and capital for the organizations' operations and supporting activities. On a day-to-day basis, it manages the company's financial reporting back to its management and shareholders. It may also manage the payroll, bookkeeping and accounts payable and receivable.

Typical Career Path

A finance professional typically starts of his or her career as an analyst, taking part in producing financial reports and projections. They also consult in budget creation and ROI suggestions for senior management. As they gain experience, a financial analyst can expect to move into a senior analyst role or into a managerial or a program manager position. In most finance positions, a bachelor's degree is required, and many professionals also attain an MBA.

Organizational Motivation

Finance is interested in the uninterrupted financial health of the company. All financial managers are responsible for the fiduciary stewardship of the organization that best benefits the company's owners and shareholders. It is also a finance department initiative to maintain the company's credit rating so that the company has no problem obtaining interim financing from financial institutions.

Where your Organizational Motivation Overlap

As the old cliché goes, "Love and money make the world go round." While there may not be much of the former lost for finance departments by engineers who simply want to get their projects done as efficiently as possible and be compensated for it without having to justify every expense or face budget cuts, the latter nonetheless drives everything from the scope of your projects to their priority levels and how much you should be paid for them.

Simply put: finance controls the money, which is what you need in order to get anything done.

There is a lot of alignment in strategy in common with engineering, as you may be taking direction from finance in terms of cost center budgeting or cost savings goals. If you oversee specific financial deliverables, you are ultimately responsible for ensuring your projects stay on task, schedule, and budget. As the project is in progress, you may report into a member of the finance department to confirm that you are on track or have met your goals for the year.

Many people move into managerial roles within their organizations in order to have greater control over the types and scopes of projects their department will be working on. They then develop difficult relationships with the people who control the purse strings, viewing them as obstacles to securing the budgets they need to meet their goals. From the finance department's perspective, yours is but one of countless spending requests, each of which needs to be assessed based on their potential return on investment. Unless you can convince finance that you deserve a greater share of the company budget for your work, you'll find it a perpetual challenge to secure enough funding to staff your department, execute your projects, and lead your team. It is best to keep a positive relationship with your stakeholders in finance.

HR

Human Resources works with the business to keep the company on top of labor relations, employment law, talent acquisition, employee benefits, development programs, company culture, human capital deployment, and performance management, amongst other things.

Typical Career Path

The HR career path varies by company and organization.

The HR coordinator or analyst is an entry-level position that usually requires a bachelor's degree or a college degree in a related field of study. This role helps facilitate various HR processes, including completing administrative paperwork for new hires, handling benefits plans, changes to employment or position status, including promotions, title changes, termination, and other tasks. They may be tasked with sending memos and reminders, organizing company events, and interview coordination.

The next step up is the HR Recruiter who assists the HR department with recruiting, payroll, and employee records. They are responsible for looking for the talent needed within the company to meet company goals. They arrange interviews, check references, maintain records and help with onboarding.

Next in the management chain within the HR department is the HR Manager. There is a trend for companies to hire employees as a generalist or senior generalists rather than hiring them as HR managers directly. These individuals are responsible for all parts of HR–hiring, training, benefits, payroll, compliance, and a range of other things.

Organizational Motivation

The goal of human resources is to ensure the organization has the right talent to meet its organizational goals. This includes hiring talent, assessing the market rate for this talent, managing the benefits and other perks. They also support employee discipline, serving as a subject matter expert, a witness, or a sounding board to managers. Should you leave the company, they would typically be your main contact if you need information or references or backup proving your employment. You should know that your human resources partner or key contact is not an alternative to your manager. They are only equipped to follow up to execute your manager's requests concerning their plans for you.

Where your Organizational Motivation Overlap

If an HR resource was a part of your hiring, they would want to know that they did a good job with filling your role and that their advice to your manager was sound and that they had good instincts with your hire. At this stage, they may go out of their way to help you set up administratively. Otherwise, most single contributors may rarely professionally see their HR resources for the rest of their tenure within that company.

If you become a manager, you may find yourself assigned an HR resource to help you with your hiring, firing, and resourcing concerns. They may write your requisitions for new employees or help you put your employees on an improvement plan.

IT

The Information Technology (IT) department manages the creation, monitoring and maintenance of a company's technology systems and interconnection with internals and externals services. They make build or buy decisions for new services, based on the company's present and future IT needs.

Typical Career Path

IT comprises multiple career paths, and its major categories are software, infrastructure, development, or support. For software, these can be professionals who develop, configure, or maintain the operating systems that employees use. Most of them start at an entry-level Software Development or Analyst Programmer role. They then move to a senior developer or programmer role before advancing to a project manager or consultant role.

The infrastructure department helps put in place the hardware needed for everyday use, such as the servers, the computers, and the security systems. Lastly, there are IT professionals who are hired as internal service representatives to help users with day-to-day concerns such as access, logins, system issues, and upgrades.

Organizational Motivation

The software and hardware sides of IT are incentivized to complete a project on time, on budget, and as future-proofed as possible. They loathe poor business requirements and will work with operations and engineering to ensure as little re-work as possible.

IT is interested in resolving issues at the root cause quickly. Any of those on IT operations have KPIs that require them to service a certain amount of tickets per shift or within a specific time frame.

Where your Organizational Motivation Overlap

IT and engineering departments have common goals and objectives. Depending on whether the IT individual is a software, hardware, or support, they have different organizational motivation. Sometimes the software developers may work hand in hand with engineering on a project after you and your team complete the design and other times where IT is far from engineering concerns and you may only see IT for service issues.

The only area where there may be motivational opposition may be in areas in service where engineering may want to take their time to review to root cause, however, IT Service representatives are incentivized to work quickly due to their KPI benchmarks.

Leadership Team

The leadership team in a company is the top management team made up of the VPs and C-level executives (CEO, COO, CIO). They are responsible for setting the overarching strategy, culture and motivation of the company. The leadership team also act as representatives for the company within their industry and beyond.

Typical Career Path

The leadership team tends to be made up of the highest-ranking executive in each department. They would have likely moved up through single contributor and middle management ranks, including manager and director roles, until achieving the executive title. Some have also worked as leaders in multiple departments to get a strong sense of the business or industry before moving to this step in their career.

Organizational Motivation

The leadership team's motivation is to meet the expectations of the board of directors and the investors. All initiatives that are put forth from the leadership team to support these goals would then be cascaded down to the different departments for execution.

Where your Organization Motivation overlap

The leadership team would rarely have the opportunity to be a part of the daily execution of projects. The best way for you to support the leadership team is to exceed expectations within your own department and the goals your manager set with you.

Putting it Together

This section reviewed the different departments outside of engineering that you may encounter throughout your career. As you learn to manage your contributions and role within the engineering teams, you will be given more and more responsibility to interact with and represent your team in front of your peers within the rest of the organization. Understanding their motivations and incentives will help you protect the interests of your team.

Reflection Time

Exercise: Which of the departments listed below do you interact with? What is the quality of the relationship you have with the individuals in that department? List out any specific situations here.

Department	Rate your relationship with that department from 1 to 5, with 5 being a strong relationship	Why?
Operations		
Sales		
Marketing		
Finance		
HR		
IT		

Do you have any sponsors within those departments? We will use this for future exercises in Chapters 6 and 7.

Department	Sponsor	Describe your relationship
Operations		
Sales		
Marketing		
Finance		

HR		
IT		

Now pick one of your sponsors from the other departments. How would you perceive their personalities?

Big 5 Personality Traits	Their Score
Conscientiousness	
Agreeableness	
Neuroticism	
Openness	
Extraversion	

Based on the insights in this chapter, what can you improve on in the next 30, 60 and 90 days?

Chapter Topic	30 Days Due Date:	60 Days Due Date:	90 Days Due Date:
Chapter 5 – How the other departments work *Prompt: What can you do to improve your understanding of the operations, sales, Marketing, Finance,*			

Human Resources, or IT departments?			

CHAPTER 6

The Big 5 Personality Traits for each Department

>————————————<

We have now reviewed the engineering career path and Big 5 Personality Traits and discussed an overview of all the major departments in your company. Let us now look at the Big 5 Personality Traits of each of the departments.

The amazing thing about social media is the availability of rich language data in the public realm for study. In the past several years, different academics have used data from Twitter to understand group sentiments and other psycho-social pulse readings on a population. One of the more interesting uses of Twitter data is analyzing the Big 5 Personality Traits by declared professions.

Twitter has made available a large dataset of over 1000 professions and their average rating for the Big 5 Personality traits - Openness, Conscientiousness, Extraversion, Agreeableness, and Neuroticism– along with other characteristics such as degree of hedonism, self-enhancement, and self-transcendence.

While this information is not fully conclusive, as it only draws upon users on social media, this exciting data allows us to aggregate the viewpoints and infer personality traits of a large swath of professions. This data can then be analyzed to understand the average personality of the different groups within an organization.

The caveat on this data is that there is pre-selection on Twitter users – this can have biases towards people with internet accessibility and comfort with digital technologies and may emphasize specific geographies and income levels. Nevertheless, this is incredible data to enhance our understanding of the personalities of those who work around us.

Operations

Within the Twitter Personality Data, the titles associated with operational staff range from Vice President of Operations to Operations Specialist. Within this group, there is some variability based on positions.

Here is the comparison between an average operations team member and an engineering team member. Note that the scale ranges from 0 to 1, where 0 is less indicative of the personality trait and 1 is the most indicative.

Profession	Openness	Conscientiousness	Extraversion	Agreeableness	Neuroticism
Operations	0.6354	0.5961	0.6801	0.3818	0.6527
Engineer	0.7391	0.3655	0.3370	0.1066	0.5746

Based on this data, the typical engineer is more open to new experiences but less conscientious, extraverted, agreeable, and neurotic. What may surprise some engineers is that the typical operations team is twice as extraverted than a typical engineer and three times as agreeable. This has a lot of implications for how an engineer should approach operational staff.

Quality

Profession	Openness	Conscientiousness	Extraversion	Agreeableness	Neuroticism
Quality	0.6500	0.4690	0.4954	0.2968	0.5654
Engineer	*0.7391*	*0.3655*	*0.3370*	*0.1066*	*0.5746*

Within the Twitter Personality Data, the roles within the quality department include quality control, quality manager and director of quality. There are also quality roles that overlap the engineering world, including quality engineer and software quality engineer.

There is a larger overlap between the engineering personality and the quality personality, with a quality professional being less open and neurotic than an engineer while being more conscientious, extraverted and agreeable.

Sales

The titles reflected within the Sales team includes Sales Vice President, Account directors, Sales trainers, and even Sales analysts.

Profession	Openness	Conscientiousness	Extraversion	Agreeableness	Neuroticism
Sales	0.5883	0.6194	0.7613	0.3358	0.6882
Engineer	0.7391	0.3655	0.3370	0.1066	0.5746

Unsurprisingly, extraversion has a large correlation with sales performance, but it did not have the highest correlation. Conscientiousness is the most important factor in sales performance. A Harvard Business School article found that 85% of top salespeople had high levels of conscientiousness, described as having a strong sense of duty and being responsible and reliable. This article also found emotional stability, openness, and agreeableness are not a requirement for sales performance.

Marketing

Within the Twitter Personality Data, there is a broad range of marketing-related titles, including traditional marketing titles, such as marketing strategist, Director of Marketing, and Marketing directors. There are also many newer, digital-related job titles, such as Digital Marketing Strategists, including some specific titles like Web Marketing Strategists and Email Strategists.

Profession	Openness	Conscientiousness	Extraversion	Agreeableness	Neuroticism
Marketing	0.6447	0.6151	0.7285	0.3171	0.7190
Engineer	0.7391	0.3655	0.3370	0.1066	0.5746

Again, we are seeing a pattern where engineers are high on openness, but are less conscientious, extraverted, agreeable, and neurotic than the average marketing team member.

Finance

Since finance is a broad term for a large industry, it is hard to pinpoint the exact characteristics of the big five.

Profession	Openness	Conscientiousness	Extraversion	Agreeableness	Neuroticism
Finance	0.6467	0.5402	0.6608	0.3207	0.6312
Engineer	0.7391	0.3655	0.3370	0.1066	0.5746

Overall, finance workers again have higher extraversion and agreeableness than the typical engineer.

Human Resources

Profession	Openness	Conscientiousness	Extraversion	Agreeableness	Neuroticism
HR	0.6558	0.6304	0.7567	0.4617	0.6545
Engineer	0.7391	0.3655	0.3370	0.1066	0.5746

Once again, we see engineers are more open to experiences, while being less conscientious, extraverted, agreeable, and neurotic.

IT

Here is the Twitter Personality Data summary for the IT profession.

Profession	Openness	Conscientiousness	Extraversion	Agreeableness	Neuroticism
IT	0.6729	0.6455	0.5491	0.2553	0.7216
Engineer	0.7391	0.3655	0.3370	0.1066	0.5746

This is potentially a surprising result for engineers, as engineers often think of IT workers to be closest aligned to their own personalities.

Yet again, engineers are found to be less conscientious, extraverted, agreeable, and neurotic than the average IT worker. While the typical IT workers are still more extraverts and agreeable than the engineering team, then are less so in comparison to the rest of the departments.

Putting it Together

Here is a summary of all the Big 5 Personality Traits for all the departments.

Profession	Openness	Conscientiousness	Extraversion	Agreeableness	Neuroticism
Sales	0.5883	0.6194	0.7613	0.3358	0.6882
HR	0.6558	0.6304	0.7567	0.4617	0.6545
Marketing	0.6447	0.6151	0.7285	0.3171	0.7190
Operations	0.6354	0.5961	0.6801	0.3818	0.6527

Finance	0.6467	0.5402	0.6608	0.3207	0.6312
IT	0.6729	0.6455	0.5491	0.2553	0.7216
Quality	0.6500	0.4690	0.4954	0.2968	0.5654
Engineer	0.7391	0.3655	0.3370	0.1066	0.5746

When you put all the tables together, you quickly realize that engineers seem to belong to their own class of personalities compared to the rest of the workforce. Overall, they are a little more open and less neurotic than their colleagues, however; they are about half as conscientious, half as extroverted, and a third as agreeable compared to the rest of the organization.

This information is helpful, as it will help you recognize the different ways your actions and methods are interpreted by your peers. Think about this from the other departments point of view. How would you feel if there is a department that is habitually less extraverted and agreeable than everybody in your department? Can this new thinking help you communicate better?

It is important to note again that individuals are still individuals and there is a lot of variability between personalities. It doesn't mean all engineers or IT, or sales team members have the same personality within their subgroup.

Story Time

Let's revisit our heroes from the beginning of our journey, with a focus on Chris.

Chris has had a great 10 year run as an engineering executive. He has now been promoted to the Head of Operations and the transition has hit him hard. Whereas his engineering and quality teams were a natural fit for him, his new operations teams seem to never click. Every attempt Chris makes to engage with the team just results in stilted answers and eye rolls. Chris needs to succeed in this role for him to reach his ambitious goal of being the Chief Operations Officer of a Fortune 500 company. With all the issues he has been having, his attention is no longer on his lofty goal, but on whether he will be able to keep his current job! What can he do to improve this situation?

Exercise: In the departments listed below, how would you describe Chris' relationship with his teams?

Department	Rate Chris' relationship with that department from 1 to 5, with 5 being a strong relationship	Why?
Operations		
Engineering		

Big 5 Personality Traits	Engineering Score	Operations Score

Conscientiousness		
Agreeableness		
Neuroticism		
Openness		
Extraversion		

Given what we now know about the differences between the personalities of operations and engineering, what can Joe do to help connect with his operations team? What should his next steps be?

Reflection Time

Looking at one of your sponsors from the other departments in chapter 5, how would you perceive their personalities in terms of their Big 5 Personality Traits?

Big 5 Personality Traits	Their Score	Their Department Score
Conscientiousness		
Agreeableness		
Neuroticism		
Openness		
Extraversion		

Based on the above, what have you found that works when collaborating with that group?

_____

_____

_____

Is there anything you would change about how you interact with that group?

_____

_____

_____

Let's switch gears and look at one of your detractors from the other departments in chapter 5. How would you perceive their personalities in terms of their Big 5 Personality Traits?

Big 5 Personality Traits	Their Score	Their Department Score
Conscientiousness		
Agreeableness		
Neuroticism		
Openness		
Extraversion		

Based on the above, what have you found that works when collaborating with that group?

_____

_____

_____

Is there anything you would change about how you interact with that group?

_____

_____

_____

_____

Based on the insights in this chapter, what can you improve on in the next 30, 60 and 90 days?

Chapter Topic	30 Days Due Date:	60 Days Due Date:	90 Days Due Date:
Chapter 6 - The Big 5 Personality for each departments *Prompt: What can you do to improve your relationship with the members of the operations, sales, Marketing, Finance, Human Resources, or IT departments?*			

CHAPTER 7

Developing Your Verbal Communication

In the previous chapters, we have discussed the key components of the responsibilities of a manager and areas where engineers excel and areas where they can improve. We then reviewed the typical career path of an engineer and their Big 5 Personality Traits. We reviewed a summary of the non-engineering departments within a typical company and their average Big 5 Personality Traits. We discovered that the average engineer has personality characteristics that are wholly different from the rest of the company. These differences may be hindering you from your career goals.

Now that we have statistical data on the differences in personality between engineers and other departments, we are going to work on bridging these gaps through improving your communication style.

So why is this important?

You need to be able to pick up on certain non-verbal cues and mannerisms in the workplace to be successful in the workplace. Socializing is a part of life. No matter who you are with, you will send and receive social cues and clues. Sixty to ninety percent of our communication is non-verbal so it is imperative to pay attention to not only what your coworkers are saying but also to how they are saying it.

Cues and Clues

Social cues and clues are equivalent to a language that is layered over what is actually being said. If you are struggling to get taken seriously at work despite strong technical competence, you may be missing important cues and clues that can help you communicate better with different groups and personalities.

There are two categories of social cues and clues - verbal and non-verbal signals.

Let's start with looking at verbal signals.

Verbal signals
Communication

Imagine you have put together the absolute best solution for a problem that is ailing a client. You write the proposal in an email to your boss and wait with abated breath. Why this is something that may even get you a promotion! You get no response the first day and by the end of the second day, you go to her office. Your manager looks confused and then after you explain the contents of your email again, she realizes which email you are talking about. She gives you feedback on describing the situation with more clarity, with better headings and visual aids and edits your email to about half its length before she sends it off to the client. You are shaken by the experience – why didn't your email make sense the way you wrote it?

Engineers that can clearly communicate objectives, data analysis, conclusions, and recommendations are a rarity and will certainly get promoted. Effective communication allows engineers to communicate in technical, business, or casual discussions and minimize re-work in communication.

It is important to remember that different people within your organization and outside of your organization have different levels of interest and understanding of the details your team provides. For example, the finance team may only be interested in the financial risks and rewards of the solution you designed. Likewise, the operations team may only be interested in learning how to practically implement your work and the impacts your solution has on their schedule. You must tailor your message to your audience to be successful.

Empathy

How you make others feel matters.

There is a quote that I love: "If you have something nice to say, say it all and on paper." People don't remember what you say, but how you made them feel. In the workplace, this is a vital concept.

When you show people you care, by remembering details about their personal lives, such as birthdays, the names of their partners and kids, special events they are looking forward to, and support them through difficult times such as health issues and deaths in the family, it would greatly improve your relationship at work. Don't be afraid to take that extra 5-10 minutes a day to get to know someone.

Phrasing

Phrasing is the way an idea is expressed or vocalized into words. While many engineers are excellent at putting together data analysis, some have difficulties with long form writing. Good phrasing reads clearly and succinctly, awkward phrasing typically means there is something *off* about your wording.

Knowing what to say does not come easy to most. But, luckily there are many tricks to ensure that your written work has clear phrasing, such as reading your work out loud or having a friend or a manager read your work.

Tone

Tone comprises the inflection, pitch, articulation, and volume of their speech. Tone colors a sentence and can change its nature. The tone of a communication is just as important as the content of the statement. It delivers the most cues to the listener and helps them understand whether you are serious, humorous, feeling aggrieved, or frustrated. It is important to use a tone appropriate to the message and your relationship with that person.

Attitude

How you choose to show up sets the stage for the rest of your career. Attitude describes the way a person's opinion of a subject shows up in their behaviour. Practically at work, it is the way you present your feelings about your responsibilities and your coworkers to others.

I have a personal example where I had gotten moved to a new project and my boss had to partition my responsibilities among different employees. She sends out an email to the team dividing the responsibilities. One person immediately emailed the team back complaining about the change, while another employee emailed back asking if this would be easier if she took this entire workstream on. As well, she sent me a personal message asking if I was ok as she didn't know the reason why my work was being partitioned. The attitude between the two team members was drastic, and it stuck with me for a long time.

I know it is easy to read this and start poking holes in this—maybe the other person was more swamped (he wasn't), maybe the person with the good attitude had more training (she didn't). Just step back and assume all other things are equal—who would you rather have on your team?

Putting it Together

In the previous chapter, we revealed that the average personality of an engineer is half as extraverted and a third as agreeable than the rest of the organization. If an engineer is unaware of this situation, he or she may miss signals to help them fit better into a group. These verbal clues and cues are invaluable in bridging the gaps between you and your peers. Being sensitive to your communication styles, showing empathy at work, using appropriate phrasing and tone, and having an appropriately positive attitude will help you build allies in your company and take you far in your career.

In our next chapter, we will continue our review by looking at non-verbal communication.

Story Time

Let's revisit our heroes from the beginning of our journey, returning our focus to Sarah.

Sarah thought she was doing everything right. Her boss loves her and, after finding success as a junior engineer, and in project and product management, she was given an engineering team to manage. From day one, she set strong standards on how the work should be done based on management techniques that were effective in her previous roles, but she is struggling with her new position. Each engineer needs so much of her time to train to her high standards and there are times when she just wants to stop explaining and finish the work herself. She can envision the solution so easily; why can't her employees? She cannot seem to get a good understanding of why her employees do not seem to have the same spark as she does for the work.

Her first project was a success, meeting all milestones and KPIs with gusto, but she can sense something was wrong with the team by the second and third major projects. Somehow, morale is not where it should be, and people are lackluster at team-building events. She gets her first 360-degree performance review from her team and the anonymous feedback was atrocious - not one person said anything positive about her as their manager. Worst yet, she is sure that she knows who wrote each comment. She does not know if she can treat her employees the same after what they wrote about her. Over the course of six months, she loses several star employees and she is unable to fill the role internally. She needs to turn this team around and fast.

In this story, on a scale of 1 to 5, how would you rate Sarah and her team in the following non-verbal communication skills?

Non-Verbal Communication Skill	Sarah's rating	Engineering department rating
Communication		
Phrasing		
Environmental factors		
Phrasing		
Tone		
Attitude		

How have these improvement areas contributed to the breakdown in communication between Sarah and her team?

Reflection Time

On a scale of 1 to 5, how would you rate yourself in the following non-verbal communication skills?

Verbal Communication Skill	Self-Rating	Engineering department rating	Other department ratings
Communication			
Phrasing			
Environmental factors			
Phrasing			
Tone			
Attitude			

Let's revisit your sponsors and detractors from the different departments again. What are some Verbal Cues to improve on to improve your relationship with each group?

Department	Sponsor	Verbal Cues to Improve on
Operations		
Sales		
Marketing		
Finance		

HR		
IT		

Department	*Detractor*	*Verbal Cues to Improve on*
Operations		
Sales		
Marketing		
Finance		
HR		
IT		

Do you see any trends?

_____

_____

What is something you can improve on in the next week to improve your relationship with others?

_____

_____

For your second exercise: of the areas where you said you faced difficulty in chapter 1, which of the areas listed above were related to your struggles? Why do you think it has led to tension?

_____

_____

Chapter Topic	30 Days Due Date:	60 Days Due Date:	90 Days Due Date:
Chapter 7 - Verbal Signals *Prompt: What can you improve upon in your communication, empathy, phrasing, tone, and attitude?*			

CHAPTER 8

Developing Your Non-Verbal Communication

>————————<

In the previous chapters, we learned about how different departments have different motivations and communication needs than those of the engineering department. We next discussed how to bridge that communication gap using verbal signals make a big impression on your audience. We also reviewed how to assess which skills are important in managing your team and providing effective communication with the rest of the business.

There is another sub-category of Communication Cues and Clues that are not communicated through speech but are still very powerful. These are known as non-verbal signals.

Let's dive right in!

Non-verbal Signals

Eye Contact

Let's say you were meeting someone for the first time, and she was continually looking away from you. How would you feel? Would you start questioning what you were saying? What would you think of her interest in the conversation?

It is important to maintain an appropriate level of eye contact with the person or larger audience you are speaking to. Not making eye contact may be misinterpreted as a symptom of lack of attention, anxiety or insecurity. In some cultures, it may even be seen as a sign of dishonesty.

Many people ask how eye contact should be managed if you are speaking to a crowd. The best practice is to switch your focus to different people in the audience for each sentence or major point. This will ensure your whole audience is engaged.

Expressions

Expressions count when speaking. Your facial expression is subconsciously tied to your true emotions and your audience is continuously monitoring for an alignment between your expression and the content of what you are saying. For example, if your manager is saying something positive while looking upset, there is a good chance that you don't believe that the news she is conveying is truly positive.

As discussed in Chapter 1 and 2, a manager oversees the energy of the team. As a manager, you need to ensure that you show positive energy and enthusiasm with your facial expressions by allowing your face to be animated and smiling as you talk. This will help your team be engaged in their mission.

Attention

One of the toughest things I had to learn was how to actively listen and pay attention. When I started my career, I spent a lot of my time trying to prove myself and not really paying full attention to what others are saying. This habit didn't make me a lot of work allies and made me less effective at my responsibilities in general.

I ended up taking a workshop on active listening and it was eye opening. Listening and showing that you are listening help me bridge a lot of gaps. Listening to employees, managers, and others helped me understand my work and find holistic ways to meet and exceed my responsibilities.

What are the key components of active listening? Firstly, listen without interrupting. Let the other person speak and their ideas breathe without jumping to conclusions or planning your rebuttal. Secondly, stay focused on the content and context of what they are saying and insure you note non-verbal clues and cues too. Ensure that your own non-verbal clues and cues indicates your interest and care in the discussion. Lastly, summarize to the speaker what you heard.

Try this tomorrow with your family, friends or coworkers and note how this changes your communication!

Body Posture

The positioning of your body is also used by your audience to understand your intent. For example, if you notice a coworker slouching while listening to a meeting, you may assume that he is having a tough day and not actively listening.

Poor body posture can also indicate a lack of attention or involvement during a conversation. If a person you are speaking to is leaning forward, they are signaling they are focused, attentive, and engaged in the conversation.

Fidgeting is another type of body language that people notice. Do you bite your nails, play with your pen or shake your knee? This can express to your coworkers that you are disinterested, nervous, bored, or dishonest. The next time you have a conversation, take note of your posture. What is your body posture conveying to your audience?

Energy Level

Imagine that you were a manager. You have two equally educated and experienced employees. One has a high energy level, the other does not. Who would you enjoy working with more?

I know it is easy to say that if you were the manager, then attitude would not matter, only the work would matter. But think about this from your manager's point of view. You would like some work to be done and one employee is easygoing and fun to work with while the other complains all the time. You would naturally start gravitating towards the more pleasant employee. Over time, that gravitation turns into opportunities, and promotions.

Studies have shown that difficult people bring down the morale of the entire group, even if the difficult individual was a star contributor. All the other members of the team perform better when the difficult employee leaves.

For your next meeting, try to notice your energy level in comparison to your colleagues and managers. If you have the opportunity to be in meetings with executives, compare the energy levels between the different speakers. How does each person make you feel?

Dress and Grooming

As a young manager, the most difficult conversation that I ever had was speaking to an employee who got a complaint about his personal hygiene. This was an issue, as this employee had a job where he had to frequently sit with other employees in close quarters for projects. Being a new manager, I was afraid to discuss this with the employee and researched on the internet and asked my boss and my mentors what to do. Ultimately, no matter how many articles I read and how many other managers I asked, it fell on me to deliver the message.

As an employee, you need to know that you are working with and around other people. These people will prefer working with people who are hygienic and well-groomed. If you do not meet their expectations, they may complain to your manager as my employee had experienced.

What is well-groomed? It doesn't have to mean that you look like you are about to walk off the pages of a magazine. It means that you and your clothes are both washed and of an appropriate cut that allows you to fit into your workplace environment or the occasion.

I find engineers are abrasive towards the idea that their work cannot speak for itself and would not look at this situation like that. Imagine that your work is the foundation of a building, and your appearance is the trim that goes on it. The Pantheon is beautiful because of both its engineering marvel and its handsome proportions. These qualities don't have to exist separately.

Putting it together

We have now reviewed both verbal and non-verbal cues. Together, these are powerful tools that will help you engage your peers more effectively and bridge the personality gap we noted in chapter 5. Non-verbal clues and cues are physical behaviours such as eye contact, expressions, attention, posture, energy level and hygiene and grooming help you provide stronger context to what you are communicating to your friends, family and colleagues.

Story Time

Let's revisit our heroes from the beginning of our journey, with a focus on Chris.

Chris has had a great 10 year run as an engineering executive. He has now been promoted to the Head of Operations and the transition has hit him hard. Whereas his engineering and quality teams were a natural fit for him, his new operations teams seem to never click. Every attempt Chris makes to engage with the team just results in stilted answers and eye rolls. Chris needs to succeed in this role for him to reach his ambitious goal of being the Chief Operations Officer of a Fortune 500 company. With all the issues he has been having, his attention is no longer on his lofty goal, but on whether he will be able to keep his current job! What can he do to improve this situation?

In this story, on a scale of 1 to 5, how would you rate Chris and her team in the following non-verbal communication skills?

Non-Verbal Communication Skill	Sarah's rating	Engineering department rating
Eye Contact		
Expressions		
Attention		
Body Language		
Energy Level		
Dress and Grooming		

How have these improvement areas contributed to the breakdown in communication between Sarah and her team?

Reflection Time

On a scale of 1 to 5, how would you rate Chris in the following non-verbal communication skills?

Non-Verbal Communication Skill	Self-Rating	Engineering department rating	Other department ratings
Eye Contact			
Expressions			
Attention			
Body Language			
Energy Level			
Dress and Grooming			

Let's revisit your sponsors and detractors from the different departments again. What are some Non-Verbal Cues to improve on to improve your relationship with each group?

Department	Sponsor	Non-Verbal Cues to Improve on
Operations		
Sales		
Marketing		

Finance		
HR		
IT		

Do you see any trends?

_____

_____

_____

What is something you can improve on in the next week to improve your relationship with others?

_____

_____

_____

Based on the insights in this chapter, what can you improve on in the next 30, 60 and 90 days?

Chapter Topic	30 Days Due Date:	60 Days Due Date:	90 Days Due Date:
Chapter 8 - Non-Verbal Signals *Prompt: What can you improve in your eye*			

contact, expressions, attention level, body language, energy level, and dress and grooming?			

CHAPTER 9

Putting it Together

⊢————————————————⊣

We are nearing the end of our journey together. You have already learned about your role and responsibility as a single contributor and as a manager. These different roles lead to new expectations both your employer and your employees have for you.

On top of meeting the expectations of your immediate team, you must meet the expectations from other department within the company. We also discussed how the core expectations, motivations and personalities are different in each department you work with. To be able to communicate to the different personality types within a company, we looked at verbal and non-verbal communication skills that can be improved to improve your likelihood of becoming a manager.

This last chapter will now review how you can practice the skills you just learned in this book throughout your day to day life. It will review what happened to the careers of Joe, Sarah and Chris and what they worked on to get to that point. We will then finalize the action plan that we reviewed in the earlier chapters.

Are you excited about putting all your new skills to the test?

Looking back at Expectations

In chapter 1, we looked at the expectations of single contributors and managers and you rated yourself on how you are currently performing in each task.

Managers are responsible for ...	All Employees Expect	Engineering Employees Expect	Employers Expect
Ensuring their teams have everything they need to complete assigned tasks Evaluating their teams Distributing tasks Managing payroll Ensuring their team stays on budget The energy of the team Having positive relationships with their colleagues Representing their companies	Honesty Fairness Trust Respect	Even Keeled Boss Available for 1:1s Helpful Interested in their personal lives	Adaptable to operation needs Can manage large global projects Able to lead diverse teams Deep technical knowledge Ability to convert corporate goals into personal actions

in their industries Representing their industries			

When you look at these expectations, how can you use your new knowledge on the organizational motivations and Big 5 Personalities of the different departments, verbal and non-verbal cues to improve your effectiveness in each area?

What if this doesn't work?

The question that I get at this point of the journey is the concern about what you should do if you excel at all the above and you still don't get where you want to be in your career.

First, take a deep breath and let it out. You cannot control every situation. All you can do it your best and control what you can in your career, which you have already taken the first couple steps towards.

If you follow the steps in this book, you will see visible results.

Now what if you have diligently worked through the workshops and objectively improved your performance as a single contributor or as a manager and still you have not achieved the advancement you are looking for? Your next steps depend on two things: 1. Has your manager offered specific and actionable feedback on what you need to do prior to getting promotion? 2. Are there advanced postings in your company that you are interested in?

If your manager cannot provide a strong reason related to your performance why you are not eligible for a promotion and there are no positions to apply for, it is entirely possible that your organization does not have the infrastructure or growth to get you to your next step. After exceeding expectations for three or more years without a promotion, it is acceptable practice to move to a different department or organization.

Story Time

Let's start off with what our heroes did in real life.

Joe, our star engineer, realized that he did not want to become a people manager. Looking at the personality and skills required to be an engineering manager, he realized that his skills are best put forward on the technical side. Instead he put his efforts into research and development, the theoretical side of his field and gaining more public recognition. Eventually he was recognized by his peers and was invited to join a council of world class experts in his field which gave him incredible satisfaction.

Sarah, our new engineering manager, realized she had a lot of room to grow as a manager. Luckily, her boss had faith in her and gave her monthly touchpoints to help her sharpen her skills. For extra re-enforcement, she hired an executive coach and engaged an alumni mentor to help her with her people and management skills. In a couple years, her hard work paid off and she was promoted to Director of Engineering.

Chris, our operations executive, unfortunately could not regain control of his team and ultimately decided to move on to other companies within the industry. He made a lateral move to a competitor, all the while working with an executive coach to ensure he can make a great first impression with his new team. He was very successful in his new role and was ultimately head hunted to a COO role.

Do any of these endings surprise you?

_____

_____

What areas did Joe work on to improve his career?

_____

_____

_____

What areas did Sarah work on to improve her career?

_____

_____

_____

What areas did Chris work on to improve his career?

_____

_____

_____

What top 3 insights can you bring back to your career?

_____

_____

_____

Your 90-Day Plan

Based on what you learned in this book, what do you think you can improve upon in the next 30/60/90 days? Once you have written out all your goals, please write your due dates for each action.

Chapter Topic	30 Days Due Date:	60 Days Due Date:	90 Days Due Date:
Chapter 1: Understanding the Challenge *Prompt: What can you do to improve as a single contributor? What skills can you improve as a manager?*			
Chapter 2: The roadblocks facing engineers *Prompt: What can you do to engage more stakeholders in your career? What skills can you learn to improve your competency in managerial tasks?*			
Chapter 3: The Engineering Organization *Prompt: What can you do to improve your*			

understanding of the engineering organization?			
Chapter 4: The Engineering Personality *Prompt: What can you do to align your Big 5 Personality characteristics to better align with your career goals?*			
Chapter 5 - The Big 5 Personality for outside departments *Prompt: What can you do to improve your understanding of the operations, sales, Marketing, Finance, Human Resources, or IT departments?*			
Chapter 6 - The Big 5 Personality for outside departments *Prompt: What can you do to improve your relationship with the members of the operations, sales, Marketing, Finance,*			

Human Resources, or IT departments?			
Chapter 7 - Verbal Signals *Prompt: What can you improve upon in your communication, empathy, phrasing, tone, and attitude?*			
Chapter 8 - Non-Verbal Signals *Prompt: What can you improve in your eye contact, expressions, attention level, body language, energy level, and dress and grooming?*			

How will you ensure that you meet your goals?

_____

_____

_____

How will you celebrate the completion of your goals?

_____

_____

_____

Before we part ways, write how you will feel when you complete all your goals.

_____

_____

_____

Acknowledgements

I would like to thank the incredible support of my husband throughout the writing process. Without you, this book will not be possible.

I would like to thank my incredible son, Rafael. You are my greatest inspiration.

I would also like to thank my family and RT for your help in editing the book and DT, JM, RL, WLW, NG, JC, GN, the Y and S family, the TT family and JG for all the insights during the writing process.

Lastly, I would like to thank all the amazing managers I had throughout my career and my amazing mentors, RN and PK. I have learned so much from all of you.

About the Author

Rebecca Leung Comsa is a professional engineer with two decades of leadership and managerial experience.

How to start earning money in our early 20s

Starting to earn money in our early 20s can be a challenging but rewarding experience. Here are some potential topics that could be explored in an eBook on this subject:

1. Building a strong financial foundation in your early 20s

2.   Strategies for paying off student loans and managing debt

3.   Identifying and pursuing career opportunities that align with your values and goals

4.   Developing a side hustle or entrepreneurial venture to supplement your income

5.   Maximizing your earning potential through negotiation and